Addison Wesley
Science & Technology

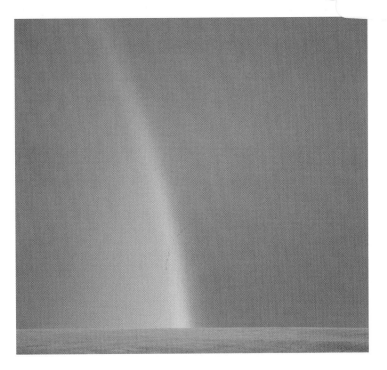

Matter and Materials
Energy and Control

•

Light

Steve Campbell

Douglas Hayhoe

Doug Herridge

Lionel Sandner

Jim Wiese

Beverley Williams

Ricki Wortzman

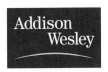

Addison
Wesley

Toronto

Coordinating & Developmental Editors
Jenny Armstrong
Lee Geller
Lynne Gulliver

Editors
Susan Berg
Jackie Dulson
Christy Hayhoe
Sarah Mawson
Mary Reeve
Keltie Thomas

Researchers
Paulee Kestin
Louise MacKenzie
Karen Taylor
Wendy Yano, Colborne Communications Centre

Consultants
Lynn Lemieux, Sir Alexander MacKenzie Sr. P.S., Toronto District School Board
Sidney McKay, Brookbanks Education Centre, Toronto District School Board
Klaus Richter, formerly Edgewood P.S., Toronto District School Board
Katherine Shaw, Miller's Grove School, Peel Board of Education

Pearson Education Canada would like to thank the teachers and consultants who reviewed and field-tested this material.

Design
Pronk&Associates

ISBN 0–201–64982–9

This book contains recycled product and is acid free.
Printed and bound in Canada.

6 – TCP – 05

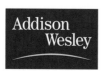

Light

Light is all around us almost all the time. But what exactly is it? Light is a form of **energy**. It travels faster than anything else in the universe. Light allows us to see colours. It also allows us to see ourselves in mirrors, to see things as larger or smaller, and even to see objects more clearly. You will be amazed by all the things light can do.

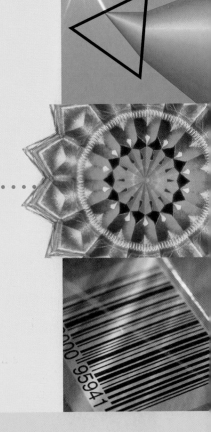

Now you will find out:

- about natural and human-made sources of light
- how light behaves as it travels and interacts with materials
- about the characteristics of light
- about shadows and how to control their shape, location, and size
- how colour is a property of light

Light in Our Lives

Get Started

Long ago the only source of light on the earth was natural light. It came from the sun, and from some types of plants and animals that glowed in the dark. Humans used the sun to guide them in their daily lives. They woke up when the sun rose and went to sleep when the sun set. They planted seeds when the days got longer. They harvested their crops when the days got shorter.

Then humans discovered how to make fire. They could now make their own light, and take control of their lives. Today, thanks to electricity, we have many sources of safe, indoor light.

Can you imagine life without light? What would a day be like in your classroom if the lights were turned off?

Work On It

1. Take a look inside and outside the house on this page. Make a list of all the light sources you can find. Decide if they are natural or **artificial** (human-made) sources of light.

2. Now imagine that the lights were turned off. Which activities do you think would have to stop and why?

3. Write or draw a picture which tells when and why the following comments might be made, either in the picture or if you heard someone say them:

   a. There's not enough light in here.

   b. We don't need all these lights on.

   c. It's too dark for you to read in this room.

   d. Don't forget to turn off the lights.

Communicate

Write

1. The light bulbs in this house all give off white light. When have you seen coloured lights in use? Why do you think coloured lights were chosen for that use?

2. Take another look at the picture of the house. Which things can you find that give off both light and heat? Which things give off only light?

3. The sun is a **light source** that we can't control. What can we do to protect ourselves from too much sunlight?

4. Make a chart with titles What I Know About Light, What I Want to Find Out, and What I learned. Add to your chart as you learn more about light.

1 How Light Travels

Can you see a **beam** of light in these two photographs?
Take a good look at the beams. How are these beams of light similar?

Work On It

The light in the photographs looks like it is travelling in a straight path. But when we see most light, it's hard to tell its path. Because sunlight and indoor lights are so bright, it's hard to see a single **ray**. In this investigation, you will be able to see clearly how light travels in a straight line.

Materials for each group:

a focussed light source (a pinpoint flashlight, a flashlight with a strong beam, or a ray box with a single slit baffle that your teacher can provide)

4 index cards   paper punch

modelling clay   drinking straw

ruler   pencil

Procedure

1 On each of the four cards, draw diagonal lines between opposite corners. The point where the two lines cross is the centre.

2 Draw a bull's-eye at the centre point on one of the cards.

3 Use a paper punch to make a hole in the exact centre of the other three cards.

4 Take four lumps of clay and place them about 15 cm apart in a straight line.

5 Stand each card up in a lump of clay. Make sure that the cards are lined up so that the centre holes are in a straight line. (You can run a straw through the holes to line the cards up perfectly.)

6 Ask your teacher to darken the room. Point the light source toward the cards so that it shines right through the holes and hits the bull's-eye.

7 Move one of the cards a little bit. Can you still see the light shining through? Explain what happened when you moved the card. What other ways can you place the cards so that the light hits the bull's-eye?

8 Draw pictures to show what you observed. Use a ruler and a sharp pencil to draw the ray of light. Include an arrowhead on the path of the light ray to show the direction the light is travelling.

Communicate Write

1. How must the cards be placed so that the light shines through the holes?

2. What have you learned about how light travels?

3. Write an explanation or draw a picture to convince someone that light travels in a straight line.

4. Look in your school, at home, or around your neighbourhood for different types of light. How are they similar? How are they different. What are they used for?

Build On What You Know

While you work on this unit, you will be creating a book full of "What If …" stories and pictures. Start with this "What If …." What would happen if the sun was our only source of light? Write a story, draw a picture or create a comic strip to explain your ideas of what life would be like.

2 Reflecting Light

Get Started

Did you know that the moon doesn't produce any light of its own? We see moonlight because the light from the sun **reflects**, or bounces, off of the moon. The moon is a source of reflected light.

There is a story that the great mathematician Archimedes used his knowledge of reflection and of how light travels to help defeat an army during the Second Punic War in 218 to 201 BC. Ancient writers say that Archimedes had soldiers line up on shore holding small mirrors. He then had them hold their mirrors to reflect the sun's light onto the Roman ships. The heat created by the reflected light was so strong that it set the ships on fire. Scientists think the idea is possible, but probably not very likely to have happened during the excitement of a battle.

Work On It

Could a large collection of small mirrors be used to aim beams of light on a distant ship? In this activity you will work with your group to investigate how light travels when it is reflected by a mirror. You can decide if you think the Archimedes story is true.

Materials for each group:

a focused light source (a pinpoint flashlight, a flashlight with a strong beam, or a ray box with a single slit baffle that your teacher can provide)

3 index cards	modelling clay
mirror ruler	pencil

Procedure

1 Draw a bull's-eye at the centre of each card.

2 Place three lumps of clay in a line about 30 cm from one another.

3 Set a target card in each lump of clay.

4 Discuss as a group where to hold the mirror and the light source so that when you shine the light on the mirror, the light reflects and hits a target. Once you have decided, draw a picture to show your idea. Label all of the objects in your picture.

5 Ask your teacher to darken the room. Test your prediction and discuss what happened. Were you successful? If not, how should you move the mirror to change the direction of the reflected ray of light?

6 Once you have been successful at reflecting the light onto one of the targets, discuss where to place the mirror to hit the other targets. In each case draw your predictions. Use a ruler to draw the light rays and show the direction the light travels with an arrowhead on each ray.

7 Keep testing your ideas until you are successful. Draw a picture that shows where to place the mirror to hit each of the targets.

Safety Caution

Be careful never to use a mirror to aim sunlight directly into someone's eyes or at dry materials such as paper or leaves that could catch on fire.

Communicate

  Write Discuss

1. You have now used mirrors to reflect light onto targets. Discuss whether you think that the soldiers you read about could have reflected light back to the ships using mirrors.

2. Light travels in a straight path, hits a mirror, and reflects off it in a straight path. Draw a picture to show this.

3. You have been asked to set up a **Laser** Game. The game will take place in the dark, and the room will have the maze shown here. Draw or trace this maze. Show where you would put mirrors so that the players could direct their lasers from the entrance of the maze to reach the exit.

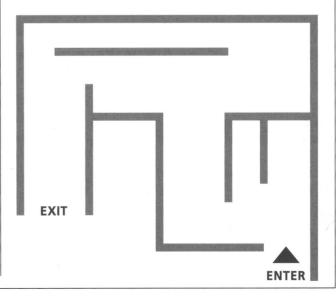

3 Good Reflectors

Get Started

We see the moon because sunlight bounces off it. In the same way, we see most things because light bounces off them. Imagine walking into a dark closet and shutting the door. You wouldn't be able to see anything. When you turn on a light, it bounces off the objects in the closet and you see them. Very few things can make their own light. Look around your classroom. What things can you find in it that make light?

Work On It

Knowing what objects are good at reflecting light can keep us safe in the dark. If you go out at night in dark clothes, other people can't see you very well. That's because dark clothes don't reflect light well.

Construction workers, police officers, and road crews often wear clothes that make it easy for people to see them. Their clothes might have strips on them that reflect light. They might also be made of materials that are good **reflectors**.

In this activity you will find out which materials make good reflectors. Test the reflecting power of a material by following the procedure.

Materials for each group:

a small mirror

lump of clay

flashlight

flat piece of foil

crumpled piece of foil

square of white paper

white card to act as a screen

square of black construction paper

squares of coloured construction paper

Procedure

1 As a group, predict which materials will be good reflectors. Arrange them in order from worst to best and record your prediction on a chart like the one shown.

Prediction		Actual Results
1.	Worst	1.
2.		2.
3.		3.
4.		4.
5.		5.
6.		6.
7.	Best	7.

2 Stand a white card in a lump of clay. This card will act as a screen.

3 Place the mirror in a spot so that when you shine a light on it, the light reflects onto the screen. (Remember what you did in the last activity.)

4 Ask your teacher to darken the room. Shine the light onto the mirror.

5 Look at the light reflected from the mirror onto the card. Notice the brightness and shape of the reflected light on the card. You will be using this to compare how each of the other materials reflects light.

6 Put the mirror down. Take turns using each of the other materials in place of the mirror.

continue...

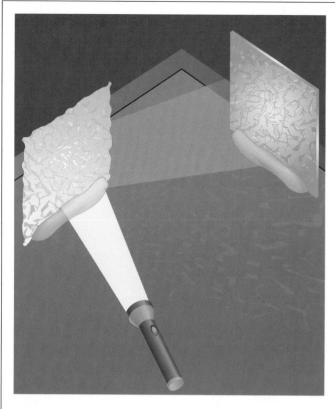

	Things That Make Their Own Light	Things That Reflect Light
Classroom		
Outside		
At Home		

7 Each time, observe how well light bounces off the material onto the screen compared to how well it bounced off the mirror. Rate each material from the worst to the best reflector on your chart.

8 Look at the predictions you made at the beginning of this investigation. How do they compare?

Communicate

Write

1. Make a chart to show Things That Make Their Own Light and Things That Reflect Light. Consider objects and materials found in your classroom, outside, and at home. Underline the human-made things listed on your chart.

2. You tested flat and crumpled foil and found that they reflected light differently. Do you think the texture of a material changes how it reflects light? Write a few sentences to explain what you think. To find out, glue different textures (crumpled, smooth, ridged, bumpy) of the same colour of paper onto cards. Then test their reflecting power. Show your results in a chart or by writing and drawing.

3. People on bikes need to be seen easily, especially when it is getting dark outside. Remember what you have learned about materials and how they reflect light. Draw a design for a bike helmet that you think would make a person easy to see in the dark. Explain what material the helmet would be made of and why you would choose this material.

4. The paint used to mark lines on road surfaces is different from house paint. Why do you think this is a better paint to use on roads than a regular house paint?

Build On What You Know

It's time for another entry in the "What If …" book. What would happen if your clothes reflected all light? Write or draw a picture or a comic strip to explain your ideas.

Building Optical Devices

Looking through a periscope

Image inside a kaleidoscope

Get Started

You have seen that mirrors are good reflectors of light. Periscopes and kaleidoscopes both make use of mirrors and their ability to reflect light.

In a kaleidoscope, several mirrors bounce light to each other and make beautiful designs. If there is an object inside the kaleidoscope that can move, a very large number of patterns can be made.

In a periscope, mirrors are used to see around corners or above the heads of people. In wartime, periscopes were used in submarines or trenches to see what was going on above without being seen. Today, we often use them for fun.

In this activity, you and your group will build a kaleidoscope, then design and build a periscope. You will learn more about how mirrors reflect light, and how reflected light allows us to see.

Build a Kaleidoscope

Materials for each group:

3 small mirrors   pen
scissors   tracing paper
small beads   tape
small piece of cardboard or Bristol board

Optional materials:
flashlight

Safety Caution

Never stare directly into a bright light or the sun.

Procedure

1 Tape the mirrors together with their shiny sides facing in to form a triangle.

2 Stand the mirrors on the cardboard or Bristol board and draw around the base.

3 Cut out the triangle you have traced and make a small hole in the middle with a pen.

4 Tape the card triangle to one end of the mirrors.

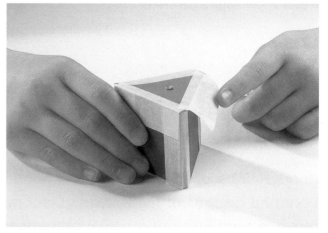

5 Tape the tracing paper over the other end of the mirrors.

6 Drop the beads through the hole in the cardboard.

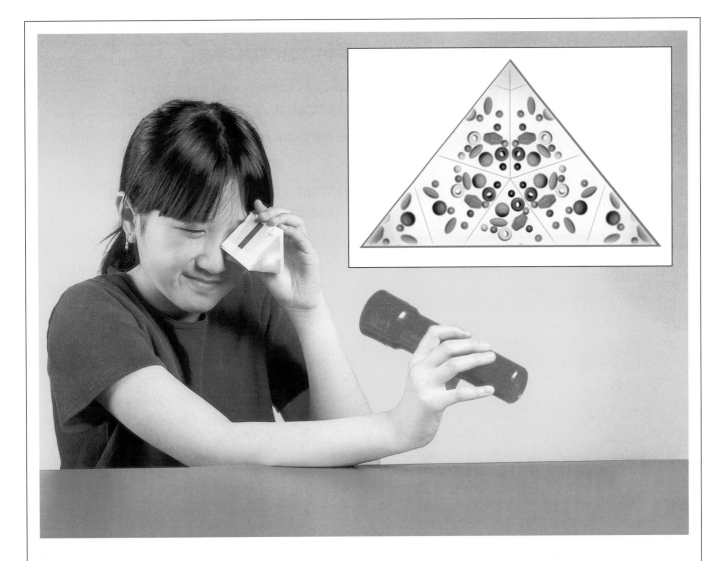

7 Aim your kaleidoscope down toward a bright light or flashlight and look through the hole.

8 Turn the kaleidoscope to change the pattern.

Design a Periscope

Materials for each group:

tape   scissors

two small mirrors   safety goggles

a clean, empty one-litre milk carton

piece of cardboard cut into a right-angled triangle to draw diagonal lines

Procedure

1 How could a periscope help you to see around a corner or over a high wall? How might you design and build a working periscope?

2 Think about how you could use the materials listed to build a periscope. How will you let light in? How will you position the mirrors? What will you need to measure to build your periscope?

continue...

3 Create a detailed plan of your periscope. Make a sketch and label all of the parts.

4 Build and test your periscope. Try looking around a corner or over a desk. Do you need to change anything to improve the way your periscope works? Make your changes and test your periscope again. Try out another group's periscope. How is it similar to yours? How is it different?

Discuss these questions with your classmates.

1. How are periscopes and kaleidoscopes similar?

2. What do you know about how light behaves with mirrors? How does this help you understand how these devices work?

3. The word kaleidoscope means "beautiful to look at." Why do think it has that name?

4. When would you find a kaleidoscope or a periscope useful?

5. How would you change your kaleidoscope or periscope if you were making a new one.

5 Transparent, Translucent, and Opaque

Get Started

People make all sorts of things from different kinds of materials. When we choose a material, we choose it because it acts in certain ways. Take windows, for example. The three windows shown here are all made from different types of glass. There is a reason for choosing each type of glass. Where have you seen windows like these? Why were they used?

Work On It

What do you think can happen when light rays hit an object in their path? The rays might pass through the object, scatter off the object, or be **absorbed** by the object like a sponge absorbs water.

Materials that let light shine through are called **transparent**. You can see through transparent objects because the light isn't scattered or stopped. Which of the windows on the previous page are transparent?

Materials that let some light through are called **translucent**. You can't see things through them very clearly. Only some light passes through them, while most of the light is scattered off them. Which of the windows on the previous page are transluscent?

Materials that block all light from getting through are called **opaque**. Opaque objects absorb or reflect light. Since opaque objects block all light from passing through them, they cast shadows.

In this activity you will have a chance to see how light behaves when it hits transparent, translucent, and opaque materials.

Materials for each group:

a flashlight

collection of materials such as waxed paper, white paper, clear plastic wrap, coloured construction paper, and other kinds of material

Procedure

1 Work with your group to plan a test to find out which materials are transparent, translucent, or opaque. For the test to be fair, you must be sure to do the test on each material in the same way.

2 Record your findings in a chart.

Materials	Transparent	Translucent	Opaque
waxed paper			
plastic wrap			

3 Decide how to present your results so other people will understand them.

Communicate

Present Discuss Write

Discuss questions 2 - 5 with your classmates. Record your answers.

1. Share your investigation and results with another group. Look at your classmates' investigation. How did they make sure that their experiment was a fair test?

2. Are clouds translucent or transparent? How would our lives be changed if clouds were opaque?

3. Water is transparent. How could you change it to make it translucent?

4. Paper is opaque. Put drops of water on a piece of paper and shine light through it. What do you notice?

5. Think of an object that is transparent. Why might you want it to be translucent or opaque? Explain.

6. Search for objects at home that you can add to your chart of Transparent, Translucent, and Opaque objects.

Build On What You Know

Add a story, picture, or comic strip to your "What If ..." book. What might happen if there were no natural materials that were opaque?

6 Casting Shadows Outside

Get Started

You have probably seen lots of shadows. Now you know why they happen—light travels in a straight line, but it can be blocked by an opaque object in its path. The blocking causes a shadow to be cast.

You are an opaque object. If you stand in front of a light, you create a shadow. Artists used to trace a person's shadow onto dark paper, and then cut it out. The finished product was a shadow portrait, or a **silhouette**.

The word silhouette comes from the name of a French politician, Etienne de Silhouette. People used to make cartoons of him because he was unpopular.

Work On It

In this activity you will go outside to see your own shadow and make your own shadow portrait. Before you go, write or draw pictures to tell what you think you already know about shadows outside.

Materials for each pair:
pencil and paper for recording
string   chalk

Procedure

1 In the morning your teacher will take you outside. Use chalk to trace your partner's shadow onto the pavement. Your partner will then trace your shadow. Label the shadows with your names.

2 Cut a string to the length of the shadow. Draw a sketch of the shadow on paper to show the shape.

3 At midday and later in the afternoon your teacher will take you outside to repeat steps 1 and 2. Before you go, draw a prediction of what your shadow will look like. Estimate the length of your shadow. When you go outside, make sure to stand in the same position each time.

4 Make a bar graph to show the change in the length of your shadow. Draw your graph by hand or with a computer.

Make a drawing to show the change in direction of your shadow in relation to the sun.

Communicate
Discuss

Discuss these questions with your partner.

1. How did your shadow change during the day?

2. Where does a shadow lie compared to the object casting the shadow and the sun?

3. When do you think your shadow will be shortest?

4. Do you think that there is a time during daylight hours when you do not have a shadow?

5. How do you think your shadows in winter compare to your shadows in summer?

7 Indoor Shadows

Get Started

Have you ever noticed how the shadow of an object can look a lot different from the actual object? Here is a simple way to use your hands to make a bird's head.

Take a look at the pairs of hands and the shadows on the following page. What animals do you see? Talk about your observations with a classmate.

Work On It

In the last activity you discovered that the position, shape, and size of a shadow changed throughout the day based on the position of the sun. Now you will find out how the distance of an object from a light source affects a shadow.

Materials for each student:

light source such as a powerful flashlight or overhead projector

screen (wall hung with large sheets of white paper)

Procedure

1 Your teacher will darken the room and set up a light source.

2 Begin by trying to make the shadows shown on this page.

3 After you have had the chance to make different shadows, someone might draw a bird cage on the screen.

4 Practice making a bird shadow like the one shown on the previous page. What is the largest possible bird you can make for this cage? What is the smallest possible bird you can make?

Communicate

Write

1. Explain where you should stand in relation to the light source to make a large shadow. Where should you stand to make a small shadow?

2. What have you learned about shadows that you didn't know before?

3. Invent some of your own shadow objects and show a friend how to create them.

8 A Bend in the Path

Get Started

Have you ever ridden in a car on the highway in the summer and seen what looks like wet pavement ahead? When you actually get to the spot, the pavement is dry. What you have seen is a **mirage**. Thanks to the way light acts when it hits warm air, people see mirages everywhere from the desert to the Arctic Ocean. Mirages appear because air doesn't always let light beams travel in a straight path. Sometimes when light hits warm air near the ground, the light bends, and makes us see something that isn't really there.

Work On It

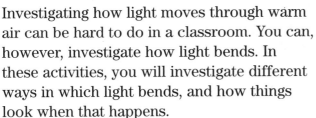

Investigating how light moves through warm air can be hard to do in a classroom. You can, however, investigate how light bends. In these activities, you will investigate different ways in which light bends, and how things look when that happens.

Your teacher might have you do all of the activities, or some groups may do certain ones and report back to the class.

Broken Pencil

> **Materials for each group:**
> glass filled halfway with water
> pencil

Procedure

1 Make sure your glass is half-filled with water.

2 Place the pencil in the glass.

3 Hold the glass at eye level.

4 Describe the pencil. Draw what you see.

Seeing Things

Materials for each group:
cup   penny

jug of water

Procedure

1 Place the cup on a desk and put the penny in it.

2 Move away from the cup very slowly until you can no longer see the penny.

3 Keep still and ask a classmate to fill the cup with water slowly so the penny is not disturbed. When do you see the coin again?

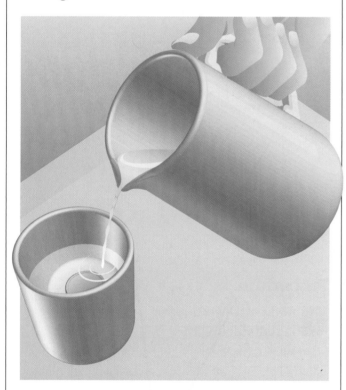

4 Take turns so that everyone sees what happens. Draw pictures or write about what you observed.

Strange Pictures

Materials for each group:
paper and markers

jar of any size, with lid

Procedure

1 Fill the jar with water and screw the lid on tight.

2 Use bright colours to draw a tree on a piece of paper. Hang your finished picture on the wall.

3 Hold the jar of water between your eyes and the picture.

4 Draw what your picture looks like.

5 Move the jar nearer to or farther away from the picture. Try turning the jar on its side or upside down. Each time the picture changes, draw a picture to show what it looks like.

Communicate
Write

1. Write a note or draw a picture to convince someone that light can bend.

2. Think about what you saw with the pencil in the glass. What do you think your legs look like when you stand in a pool of water?

3. Can you think of any other times when you have noticed light bending? Be on the lookout and ask people if they have noticed it. Record each example that you find.

9 Lenses All Around You

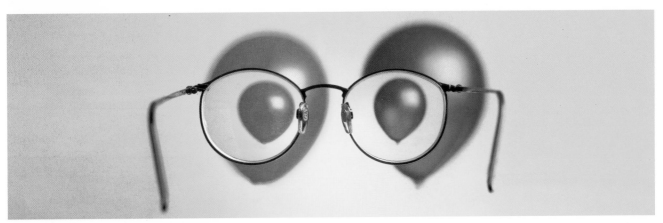

Get Started

Do you wear glasses to help you see better? If you don't, you probably know someone who does. Think about what you have learned about light bending. That should help you get the idea of how lenses work in eyeglasses. When light passes through the lens in eyeglasses, it bends. Each lens is made so that light bends to correct the person's vision.

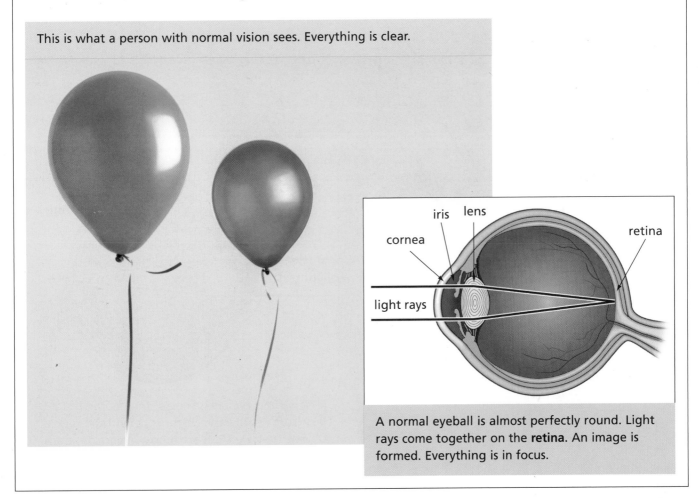

This is what a person with normal vision sees. Everything is clear.

iris   lens

cornea

retina

light rays

A normal eyeball is almost perfectly round. Light rays come together on the **retina**. An image is formed. Everything is in focus.

A **nearsighted** person sees this. Everything at the front of the picture is clear. Everything at the back is blurry.

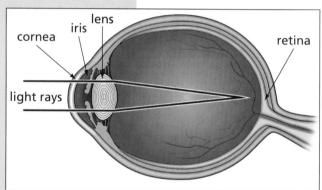

A nearsighted eyeball is longer than normal. Light rays from far-away objects come together in front of the retina, not on it. Any rays that reach the retina make for a blurry picture. Anything close to the eye is clear.

A **farsighted** person sees this. Everything at the front of the picture is blurry. Everything at the back is clear.

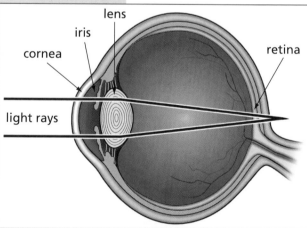

A farsighted eyeball is shorter than normal. Light rays from nearby objects focus behind the retina. Objects that are close are blurry. Objects that are farther away are clear.

Lenses can help you see better, even if they're not in eyeglasses. Scientists use **magnifying lenses** to investigate tiny or far-away objects. If you look at a magnifying lens, you will see that it is thicker in the middle than at the edges. A magnifying lens makes things look larger.

In these activities you will use a liquid to make a curved surface to form a lens. These liquid lenses bend the light rays that pass through them. The bending makes the images you see through the lenses look bigger.

Paper Cup Magnifier

Materials for each student:
container such as a paper cup
elastic band
small objects
plastic wrap
water

Procedure

1 Separate the small objects on the bottom of the container.

2 Cover the top of the container loosely with plastic wrap. Put the elastic band around it to keep the plastic wrap on.

3 Gently push the plastic wrap to make a dip in the middle.

4 Carefully pour water into the dip. Notice that the water is flat on top but curved underneath.

5 Look down into the container.

6 Observe how the water magnifies the objects.

7 Experiment to see if you can make your lens more powerful by using different containers such as a large pail.

Water Drop Lens

Materials for each student:
eyedropper
plastic wrap
newspaper
water
cooking oil

Procedure

1 Place the newspaper on the table. Cover it with plastic wrap.

2 Choose a letter or letters to magnify.

3 Using the eyedropper, release one drop of water on the plastic wrap over those letters.

4 Look at the letters. How does the size of the letters compare to the size before you added the water?

5 Repeat step 3 using a drop of oil instead.

6 What effect does the drop of oil have on the size of the letter?

Communicate
Write

1. In this lesson you made a lens to magnify objects. You read about how the lenses in eyeglasses help correct vision for some people. What other devices have lenses in them to help us see better? Make a list and share it with a classmate. Add other devices to the list as you think of them.

2. Does anyone in your family wear glasses? Is he or she nearsighted or farsighted? Examine the lenses and describe what they look like? Draw the lenses and compare them to others you have seen in this activity.

3. Interview an **optometrist** or do research to find out how different shaped lenses are used to correct eye problems. Make a poster or create diagrams on your computer to report your findings.

10 Rainbows and Prisms

Get Started

When light passes from air to water and from water to air, it does something amazing—it bends. Light also bends when it passes through a **prism**. Have you ever seen a prism? A prism is a block of glass or clear plastic. Prisms usually have rectangular sides and triangular ends. We call this shape a triangular prism. Crystal sun catchers and diamonds are both made up of triangular prisms.

Sunlight is made up of many colours of light that mix together to make white light. When light passes through a prism, it bends and we can see all the colours separately because each colour of light bends by a different amount.

When we see a rainbow, we are seeing natural prisms at work. A raindrop is a tiny natural prism. How do you think it works to make a rainbow?

Think about the times when you have seen rainbows. Rainbows happen when the air is full of moisture after a rain shower. As the sky clears and the sun comes out, a rainbow appears. This is because the drops of water are acting like tiny prisms to bend the light of the sun.

When you see a rainbow, you see the colours in separate bands. This happens because each colour of light bends a different amount when it passes through a raindrop just as it does when it passes through a glass prism.

But you don't always see a rainbow after it rains, do you? You can only see a rainbow when the sun is behind you, and falling water is in front of you. The water doesn't have to be rain, either. You can see a rainbow in the mist above a waterfall or in the drops from a lawn sprinkler.

And what about that pot of gold at the end of the rainbow? Well, rainbows are actually circles. They look like arches to us because we only see the top part of the rainbow. To see the whole circle, you would have to be in an airplane high above and looking down upon the rainbow. So, could there really be a pot of gold at the end of the rainbow?

You can make a rainbow in your classroom on any sunny day. Fill a tray with water about 3 cm deep. Place the tray of water in direct sunlight. Rest a small mirror in the water against the edge of the tray. Tilt the mirror to reflect the sunlight onto a large piece of white paper or a blank wall. Do the colours of the rainbow always apear in the same order?

Communicate

 Write

1. The colours of the rainbow are called the **spectrum**. These colours are: red, orange, yellow, green, blue, indigo, and violet. Some people remember the order by using the name "Roy G. Biv." Make up your own way to remember the order of the colours of the spectrum.

2. What conditions must happen to cause a rainbow?

3. Interview people to find out when they have seen rainbows. Record the different responses.

4. You can make a rainbow outdoors by trying the following experiment. Draw a picture of the setup, and try it when the conditions are right.

   When the sun is low in the sky, stand with your back to it. Turn on your outdoor water hose. Turn the nozzle until the spray is at its widest angle. You will see a rainbow in the water.

Build On What You Know

You're ready for the final entry in your "What If …." book. Write a story or draw a picture or a comic strip to tell about what would happen if light did not bend when it travelled from water to air. Add your book to a class collection of "What If …" books.

11 Investigating Colours

Get Started

Mixing colours is probably nothing new to you. What have you noticed when you've painted, coloured, pasted tissue paper, or mixed coloured water together?

Mixing colours of light is like mixing colours of paint. Different combinations of colours create other colours. With paint, the primary colours are red, yellow, and blue. If you mix those colours, you get other colours. With light, the primary colours are red, green, and blue. These are the three colours you mix to get all of the different colours of light.

You have learned that sunlight looks white. But when you made rainbows, you saw that sunlight is really made up of the colours of the spectrum—red, orange, yellow, green, blue, indigo, and violet. When you take these colours of light and combine them again, you create white light. Creating white light is a tricky thing to do in an experiment. But you can experiment to see how colours of light combine.

In this activity you will investigate how a piece of coloured acetate can change what other colours look like. You will also mix colours of light and make new colours.

Materials for each group:

coloured acetates (red, green, and blue)

flashlight

white paper

tape

Procedure

1 Choose a coloured acetate. Look through it at objects of different colours. What do they look like? Keep track of your observations in a chart.

Colour of Object	Acetate Colour	Predicted Colour through Acetate	Colour of Object through Acetate

2 Repeat step 1 using the other coloured acetates. Keep adding your observations to the chart.

3 Now tape one of the coloured acetates over the end of your flashlight.

4 Get together with a group that has a different-coloured acetate on its flashlight. Discuss as a group what colour you think your two groups will be able to make. Use a chart to record your prediction.

Colours Mixed	Predicted Colour	Actual Colour

5 Ask your teacher to darken the room. Then test your prediction by shining both your flashlights at the same spot on a sheet of white paper. Record your result on the chart.

6 Repeat steps 4 and 5 with other groups. Add your predictions and results to the chart. Make a note of anything that surprised you. Record any questions you have about what you observed.

Join with two other groups so that you have all three colours of light represented. Darken the room and shine your lights at the same spot on a white sheet of paper. What colour is the light?

Communicate

 Write

1. Imagine that you are looking at the blue sky through a red acetate. What colour do you think you would see? What is your prediction based on? What would the sky look like through a green acetate?

2. Suppose you were offered a pair of coloured-acetate glasses to wear. What colour would you choose for the acetate? Why?

3. The acetate only lets certain colours through. Look at the first chart you created. Record the colour of the acetate you used and then record the colour of light it lets through. (Hint: You can tell by

answering this question: If you used red acetate, what colour would you see?)

4. How can we use coloured filters in everyday life?

5. You are in charge of a light show. You can use three different colours of spotlight. Which colours will you choose? Why?

6. Use a magnifying glass to examine the screen of a colour television. The picture is made up of tiny coloured dots. What colours are these dots? These three colours combine to make all the colours you see when you watch television.

12 Inventions Using Light

Get Started

All light is a form of energy. Plants use the natural light energy from the sun to make their food. Light energy combined with photographic film produces an image that we call a **photograph**. Scientists use both natural and artificial light to do many different jobs. Light energy can make electricity, send signals, and diagnose and treat illness.

Thomas Edison is famous for inventing the light bulb. But did you know that the first light bulb was invented by Henry Woodward of Toronto, in 1874? Woodward later sold a share in his patent to Edison who improved the design.

Every day, you see things that use light energy—you just might not know that that's how those things work. Read on to find out how light energy brightens your day!

The Invisible Switch

You've probably walked through automatic doors hundreds of times. You walk up, and the door seems to open like magic. But it's not magic. There's a small cell connected to the door switch. That cell, called a **photocell**, is sensitive to light and shadows. When your shadow falls across the photocell, it triggers the door to open.

Automatic doors

Light Power

Light energy is often used to make electricity. Cells that do this are called **photoelectric cells**. A photoelectric cell that gets its light energy from the sun is called a **solar cell**. A small solar cell can collect light energy to run a calculator. A very large solar cell, or several of them, can collect a lot of light energy to make enough electricity to heat a house or a building.

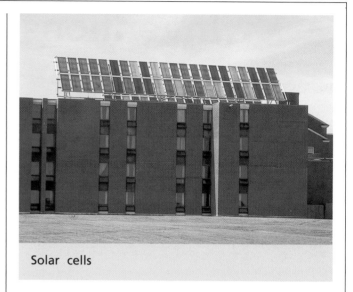
Solar cells

Light Reading

Have you seen those little black bars on things you buy at the supermarket? They might not mean much to you, but they mean everything to the beam of light at the check-out counter. A cashier passes the little black bars or **bar code** across the light beam. The beam "reads" the pattern of light and dark in the code. The pattern is checked against a computerized list. When there's a match, a signal is sent to the cash register that prints the correct name and price for the product.

Bar-code reader

Light Music

Laser light is so powerful that it can be used to drill rock or cut metal. But you might find a laser beam in your own home. A compact disc player uses a beam of laser light to play CDs. A CD has a shiny metal surface with grooves in it. In the grooves are very small bumps that make a pattern. That pattern is a code. The laser beam reflects off the surface of the disc and reads the code. It turns the code into sound.

Compact disc player

Light Conversation

You've seen telephone poles and wires. They carry our voices across the city and across the world so we can talk to one another. But those wires don't carry very many voices at once. That's why light tubes, called **optical fibres**, are used. While you talk, your voice is turned into electricity. That electricity is turned into codes of laser light flashes. Those flashes move along the optical fibre, which is about as thick as a human hair. One optical fibre can carry more than 1000 telephone messages at the same time—and it can do it much faster than regular wires.

Optical fibres

 ### If Time Allows...

Research to find out more about one of the items shown that use light energy, or find out about another one. Prepare a report to share with your classmates.

Communicate
Write

1. Write a commercial or an advertisement about one of the items shown above that uses light energy. Be sure to point out how important light is.

2. How does your family use light at home? What items in your home are based on light? Write about or draw the items you find. Look back at the illustration in the Launch activity. Can you find any more uses of light?

3. Write an acrostic about light. Write the word "Light" down the side of a page. Use each letter to tell about a way in which light is used.

Design Project

Invention Convention

Get Started

Many things that are part of our everyday life make use of how light and shadows work. Think of what you now know about light and shadows, and write down your information. Talk with your classmates and compare your recordings.

Work On It

Earlier in this unit you designed and built a periscope, a kaleidoscope, and magnifying lenses. In this project, you will design and build a new invention that uses light or light and shadows together. Your invention can be as weird and wonderful as you wish, but it should be useful in some way. It may help to think of a problem you have experienced. Then design an invention to solve this problem.

You might want to invent:

- something to help you see around corners, over fences, and in the room next door
- a tool that helps you to write in the dark
- a device that a cyclist will find safe and handy
- a new toy
- a device to help a cyclist be seen in all kinds of weather
- a system of mirrors and light that allows a clerk to see everything in a store
- a device for you to see what is going on behind you

You can then follow your plan and build your invention. You will present your finished invention at a Class Invention Convention.

Design Project

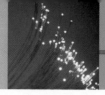

Materials for each student:

pencil and paper

variety of materials such as mirrors, tin foil, reflective tape, cardboard tubes, containers, acetate, cardboard, Bristol board, flashlights, scissors, tape, glue

Procedure

1 Think about what you want to invent. What problem will your invention solve?

2 Do some research. Search for ideas in books and around the classroom and in your home. What materials will you need to build your invention? How will you build it?

3 Choose the materials you want to use. Draw a detailed plan of your invention. Label all the parts and include a list of the materials.

4 Write a description of how the device works. Explain how light and shadows are important in your invention.

5 Build and test your invention. Do you need to change anything? How will you revise your plan? Rebuild and test your invention until you are satisfied with the way it works. Get ready for your presentation.

Communicate

Present   Write

Present your plan, explanation, and your invention at the Class Invention Convention.

1. What were the main challenges you faced in planning and building your invention? How did you deal with them?

2. Most inventors revise their plan many times before they are satisfied with their inventions. How did you have to change your plan before you were satisfied?

3. What does your invention reveal about light and shadows?

4. Create a commercial or advertisement for your invention to show how useful and special it is.

Review

Demonstrate What You Know

Get Started

Now it's time to show how much you have learned about light. Read over what your tasks are and talk to your teacher if you are unclear about what to do.

Work On It

Suppose you are camping out on an island and need to send messages during the day and at night. You need to think of a way to send signals that tell people:

- everything is fine

- you need more food

- you need help

Here are some materials that are available.

1. Design a device that allows you to send signals during the day and night. Remember that you need three different types of signals. Create a detailed drawing of the device.

2. Clearly label all the parts and write a description of how the device works. Explain the three types of signals.

3. Explain why you chose the materials you did. Would you have liked to use other materials? Which materials would you have liked to use? Why?

4. Now check your work.

   ✓ My design allows the device to send three different types of signals during the day and night.

   ✓ My design shows a detailed drawing of the device and is clearly labelled.

   ✓ My description explains how the device works.

   ✓ I have explained why I chose the materials that I did.

   ✓ My design and description explain how light can be used to send signals.

Communicate

Now it's time to think about how well you did. Use this chart to help you score your work. Four stars is the highest score for each.

1 Star ★   **2 Stars** ★★   **3 Stars** ★★★   **4 Stars** ★★★★

- **How much do you know about light? Look at your labelled drawing, list of materials, and your description of your device. Does your work show that you know**

| A little about light how light travels | Some information about how light travels | A lot of information about how light travels | All about how light travels? |

- **Look at the description of your design. Does your work show you have applied**

| A few of the skills to use light to send signals | Some of the skills to use light to send signals | Most of the skills to use light to send signals | All of the skills to use light to send signals? |

- **Now look again at your description of how the signals and your device works. Will a reader find your description**

| Not very clear or precise | Somewhat clear and precise | Mostly clear and precise | Very clear and precise? |

- **How much understanding does your design show you have about how materials transmit, reflect, or absorb light?**

| Not much understanding | Some understanding | A good understanding | A complete understanding |

Write a short note explaining how well you think you did.

Explain Your Stuff

What did you learn about light?

1. Draw an object that makes its own light. Draw an object that is a human-made source of light.

2. How do you know that light travels in a straight line?

3. Sketch a flashlight shining onto a mirror. Show how light travels after it hits the mirror.

4. Name two materials that reflect light well. Name two materials that do not reflect light well.

5. Draw and label sketches to show that you understand the following types of materials:

   a) transparent
   b) translucent
   c) opaque

6. Explain how shadows are created. Look at the illustration of the tree and its shadow shown below. Copy this sketch and show where the sun must be in the sky.

7. If there were a light source in your room shining onto a screen, where would you hold a puppet to cast a very large shadow? A small shadow?

8. What happens to light as it passes from air to water or to a solid such as glass? How do you know this?

9. Make a chart like this one and list as many things as you can that use mirrors and lenses.

Mirrors	Lenses

10. How is mixing colours of light the same as mixing colours of paint? How is it different?

Review

How Did You Do?

1. List three things you didn't know about light before the unit started.

2. Describe what you liked best in this unit. Why? What did you like least? Why?

3. Give yourself a pat on the back! What did you do well in this unit?

4. List three questions you would like answered about light.

Now you know a lot about light! Here are some of the things you've learned:

- Many objects such as the sun, a candle or a light bulb give off both light and heat.

- Some objects such as fireflies give off light but very little heat.

- Some objects such as fireflies and mushrooms that glow in the dark, and the stars make their own light.

- Most objects that produce light are artificial, rather than natural.

- Light travels in a straight line and in all directions.

- Materials can affect light. For example, air, water, and glass can cause light to bend and change direction.

- When rays of light hit a surface they may bounce back. This is called reflection. Flat, shiny surfaces produce the best reflections.

- Transparent materials like glass allow most light to pass through them. Translucent materials like tissue paper allow less light to pass through. Opaque materials absorb most light and cast shadows.

- Shadows are created because light travels in a straight line and cannot bend around corners.

- Light can be separated into a pattern of colours called a spectrum. A spectrum consists of these seven colours: red, orange, yellow, green, blue, indigo, and violet.

- Objects reflect the light that falls on them and our eyes see the reflected light. The colour of an object depends upon the colour of the light reflected back to our eyes.

- Transparent materials (water, glass, clear plastic) which can bend light work as lenses. They make things look larger or smaller depending on the shape of the lens.

- Many devices which help us in our daily lives (things like magnifying lenses, binoculars, telescopes, reading glasses) work because of the way that light behaves as it strikes lenses and mirrors.

Glossary

absorb to take in

artificial manufactured; made by humans

bar code black bars on product packages that contain product information

beam a ray of light

energy a force or power

farsighted able to see clearly far-away objects; near objects look blurry

laser a device that produces a narrow and powerful beam of light

lens a piece of clear material that bends light as it passes through it

light source origin or producer of light

magnifying lens a lens or combination of lenses that make objects look larger than they really are

mirage something you see that isn't really there; an optical illusion caused by the reflection of light by a layer of warm air

nearsighted able to see clearly near objects; far-away objects look blurry

opaque does not allow light to pass through

optical fibres long, fine glass or acrylic fibres used to transmit light

optometrist a person who examines people's eyes and prescribes lenses to correct any vision problems

photocell a small cell sensitive to light and shadows, used to trigger such things as automatic doors

photoelectric cell a device that uses light energy to make electricity

photograph an image produced by light energy combined with photographic film

prism a clear piece of glass or plastic with rectangular sides and triangular ends; used to separate white light into the seven colours of the spectrum

ray a narrow beam of light that travels in a straight line from a light source

reflect to bounce back

reflector a material that reflects light

retina part of the eyeball that is sensitive to light

silhouette an outline of someone's head cut out of black paper or filled in with a single colour

solar cell a device that changes sunlight into electricity; a kind of photoelectric cell

spectrum the colours of the rainbow: red, orange, yellow, green, blue, indigo, violet; the band of colours formed when white light is passed through a prism

transparent allows light to pass through so that anything behind it can be seen

translucent allows some light to pass through but scatters it so that anything behind it cannot be seen clearly

Acknowledgments

The publisher wishes to thank the following sources for photographs, illustrations, articles, and other materials used in this book. Care has been taken to determine and locate ownership of copyrighted material used in this text. We will gladly receive information enabling us to rectify any errors or omissions in credits.

Photography

p. 1 (centre) Adam Peiperl/First Light, p. 1 (bottom) PhotoDisc, Inc., p. 4 (left) Kharen Hill/T.W.'s Image Network, p. 4 (right) John Davies/Telegraph Colour Library/Masterfile, p. 5 Ray Boudreau, p. 7 Ray Boudreau, p. 8 Hemingway Stock Photograph, p. 11 (left) Corbis/Sandy Felsenthal, p. 11 (right) Adam Peiperl/First Light, p. 12 Ray Boudreau, p. 13 Ray Boudreau, p. 14 Ray Boudreau, p. 15 (left) PhotoDisc, Inc., p. 15 (top right) PhotoDisc, Inc., Stephen J. Krasemann/Valan Photos, p. 15 (bottom right) PhotoDisc, Inc., p. 17 (top) PhotoDisc, Inc., p. 18 Ray Boudreau, p. 19 Ray Boudreau, p. 20 Ray Boudreau, p. 21 (bottom) Dave Starrett, p. 23 Dave Starrett, p. 24 Dave Starrett, p. 25 Ray Boudreau, p. 26 Ray Boudreau, p. 27 (inset left) Science VU/Visual Unlimited, p. 27 (right) J.R. Page/Valan Photos, p. 28 Corbis/Galen Rowell, p. 30 (top) Ray Boudreau, p. 30 (bottom) Dave Starrett, p. 32 Ray Boudreau, p. 33 PhotoDisc, Inc., p. 34 (left) Al Harvey Slide Farm, p. 34 (top right) V. Wilkinson/Valan Photos, p. 34 (bottom right) © John Eastcott/YVA Momatiuk/Valan Photos, p. 35 (left) J.A. Wilkinson/Valan Photos, p. 35 (right) Owen Broad/T.W.'s Image Network, p. 39 Ray Boudreau

Illustration

Steve Attoe: p. 33, pp. 36-37
Bernadette Lau: pp. 2-3
Dave McKay: p. 9, p. 10, p. 22, p. 29, p. 41
Jun Park: p. 13 (inset), p. 32
Cynthia Watada: p. 23, p. 24
Dave Whamond: p. 6, p. 21, p. 28

Cover Photograph

PhotoDisc, Inc.